Forrest!

◆◎ THE LOCHLAINN SEABROOK COLLECTION ◎◆
Books by award-winning author Lochlainn Seabrook

A Rebel Born: A Defense of Nathan Bedford Forrest - Confederate General, American Legend (winner of the 2011 Jefferson Davis Historical Gold Medal)

Nathan Bedford Forrest: Southern Hero, American Patriot - Honoring a Confederate Icon and the Old South

The Quotable Nathan Bedford Forrest: Selections From the Writings and Speeches of the Confederacy's Most Brilliant Cavalryman

Give 'Em Hell Boys! The Complete Military Correspondence of Nathan Bedford Forrest

Forrest! 99 Reasons to Love Nathan Bedford Forrest

Everything You Were Taught About the Civil War is Wrong, Ask a Southerner! - Correcting the Errors of Yankee "History"

Honest Jeff and Dishonest Abe: A Southern Children's Guide to the Civil War

Abraham Lincoln: The Southern View - Demythologizing America's Sixteenth President

The Unquotable Abraham Lincoln: The President's Quotes They Don't Want You To Know!

Lincolnology: The Real Abraham Lincoln Revealed in His Own Words - A Study of Lincoln's Suppressed, Misinterpreted, and Forgotten Writings and Speeches

The Quotable Jefferson Davis: Selections From the Writings and Speeches of the Confederacy's First President

The Quotable Alexander H. Stephens: Selections From the Writings and Speeches of the Confederacy's First Vice President

The Quotable Robert E. Lee: Selections From the Writings and Speeches of the South's Most Beloved Civil War General

The Old Rebel: Robert E. Lee As He Was Seen By His Contemporaries

The Constitution of the Confederate States of America Explained: A Clause-by-Clause Study of the South's Magna Carta

The Quotable Stonewall Jackson: Selections From the Writings and Speeches of the South's Most Famous General

The Quotable Edward A. Pollard: Selections From the Writings of the Confederacy's Greatest Defender

Encyclopedia of the Battle of Franklin - A Comprehensive Guide to the Conflict that Changed the Civil War

Carnton Plantation Ghost Stories: True Tales of the Unexplained from Tennessee's Most Haunted Civil War House!

The McGavocks of Carnton Plantation: A Southern History - Celebrating One of Dixie's Most Noble Confederate Families and Their Tennessee Home

The Caudills: An Etymological, Ethnological, and Genealogical Study - Exploring the Name and National Origins of a European-American Family

The Blakeneys: An Etymological, Ethnological, and Genealogical Study - Uncovering the Mysterious Origins of the Blakeney Family and Name

Britannia Rules: Goddess-Worship in Ancient Anglo-Celtic Society - An Academic Look at the United Kingdom's Matricentric Spiritual Past

UFOs and Aliens: The Complete Guidebook

Christmas Before Christianity: How the Birthday of the "Sun" Became the Birthday of the "Son"

The Book of Kelle: An Introduction to Goddess-Worship and the Great Celtic Mother-Goddess Kelle, Original Blessed Lady of Ireland

The Goddess Dictionary of Words and Phrases: Introducing a New Core Vocabulary for the Women's Spirituality Movement

Aphrodite's Trade: The Hidden History of Prostitution Unveiled

Thought Provoking Books For Smart People
SeaRavenPress.com

FORREST!

99 Reasons To Love Nathan Bedford Forrest

LOCHLAINN SEABROOK
WINNER OF THE JEFFERSON DAVIS HISTORICAL GOLD MEDAL

Forrest's 191st Birthday / Civil War Sesquicentennial Edition

SEA RAVEN PRESS, FRANKLIN, TENNESSEE, USA

FORREST! 99 REASONS TO LOVE NATHAN BEDFORD FORREST

Published by
Sea Raven Press, P.O. Box 1054, Franklin, Tennessee 37065-1054 USA
www.searavenpress.com • searavenpress@nii.net

Copyright © 2012 Lochlainn Seabrook
in accordance with U.S. and international copyright laws and
regulations, as stated and protected under the Berne Union for the
Protection of Literary and Artistic Property (Berne Convention), and
the Universal Copyright Convention (the UCC). All rights reserved
under the Pan-American and International Copyright Conventions.

First Sea Raven Press Civil War Sesquicentennial Edition: August 2012
ISBN: 978-0-9858632-1-0
Library of Congress Catalog Number: 2012944267

This work is the copyrighted intellectual property of Lochlainn Seabrook and has been registered with the Copyright Office at the Library of Congress in Washington, D.C., USA. No part of this work (including text, covers, drawings, photos, illustrations, maps, images, diagrams, etc.), in whole or in part, may be used, reproduced, stored in a retrieval system, or transmitted, in any form or by any means now known or hereafter invented, without written permission from the publisher. The sale, duplication, hire, lending, copying, digitalization, or reproduction of this material, in any manner or form whatsoever, is also prohibited, and is a violation of federal, civil, and digital copyright law, which provides severe civil and criminal penalties for any violations.

Forrest! 99 Reasons To Love Nathan Bedford Forrest / by Lochlainn
Seabrook. Includes endnotes and bibliographical references.

Front and back cover design and art, book design, layout, and art by Lochlainn Seabrook
Typography: Sea Raven Press Book Design
All images and illustrations copyright © 2012 Lochlainn Seabrook
*Cover photo from James Dinkins' 1861 to 1865: Personal Recollections and Experiences
in the Confederate Army (1897). Image copyright © 2012 Lochlainn Seabrook*

The views on the American "Civil War" documented in this book *are* those of the publisher.

The paper used in this book is acid-free and lignin-free. It has been certified by the Sustainable Forestry Initiative and the Forest Stewardship Council and meets all ANSI standards for archival quality paper.

PRINTED & MANUFACTURED IN OCCUPIED TENNESSEE, FORMER CONFEDERATE STATES OF AMERICA

Dedication

To all those who love Forrest.

"Had Forrest the advantages of a thorough military education and training, he would have been the great central figure of the War."

Confederate General Joseph E. Johnson

CONTENTS

Notes to the Reader - page 9
Introduction, by Lochlainn Seabrook - page 10

Reason 1 - page 13
Reason 2 - page 14
Reason 3 - page 15
Reason 4 - page 16
Reason 5 - page 17
Reason 6 - page 18
Reason 7 - page 19
Reason 8 - page 20
Reason 9 - page 21
Reason 10 - page 22
Reason 11 - page 23
Reason 12 - page 24
Reason 13 - page 25
Reason 14 - page 26
Reason 15 - page 27
Reason 16 - page 28
Reason 17 - page 29
Reason 18 - page 30
Reason 19 - page 31
Reason 20 - page 32
Reason 21 - page 33
Reason 22 - page 34

Reason 23 - page 35
Reason 24 - page 36
Reason 25 - page 37
Reason 26 - page 38
Reason 27 - page 39
Reason 28 - page 40
Reason 29 - page 41
Reason 30 - page 42
Reason 31 - page 43
Reason 32 - page 44
Reason 33 - page 45
Reason 34 - page 46
Reason 35 - page 47
Reason 36 - page 48
Reason 37 - page 49
Reason 38 - page 50
Reason 39 - page 51
Reason 40 - page 52
Reason 41 - page 53
Reason 42 - page 54
Reason 43 - page 55
Reason 44 - page 56

Reason 45 - page 57
Reason 46 - page 58
Reason 47 - page 59
Reason 48 - page 60
Reason 49 - page 61
Reason 50 - page 62
Reason 51 - page 63
Reason 52 - page 64
Reason 53 - page 65
Reason 54 - page 66
Reason 55 - page 67
Reason 56 - page 68
Reason 57 - page 69
Reason 58 - page 70
Reason 59 - page 71
Reason 60 - page 72
Reason 61 - page 73
Reason 62 - page 74
Reason 63 - page 75
Reason 64 - page 76
Reason 65 - page 77
Reason 66 - page 78
Reason 67 - page 79
Reason 68 - page 80
Reason 69 - page 81
Reason 70 - page 82
Reason 71 - page 83
Reason 72 - page 84

Reason 73 - page 85
Reason 74 - page 86
Reason 75 - page 87
Reason 76 - page 88
Reason 77 - page 89
Reason 78 - page 90
Reason 79 - page 91
Reason 80 - page 92
Reason 81 - page 93
Reason 82 - page 94
Reason 83 - page 95
Reason 84 - page 96
Reason 85 - page 97
Reason 86 - page 98
Reason 87 - page 99
Reason 88 - page 100
Reason 89 - page 101
Reason 90 - page 102
Reason 91 - page 103
Reason 92 - page 104
Reason 93 - page 105
Reason 94 - page 106
Reason 95 - page 107
Reason 96 - page 108
Reason 97 - page 109
Reason 98 - page 110
Reason 99 - page 111

Notes - page 111
Bibliography - page 114
Meet the Author - page 115

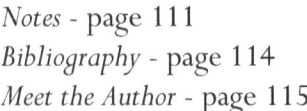

NOTES TO THE READER

☞ In any study of the "Civil War" it is vitally important to keep in mind that the two major political parties were then the opposite of what they are today. The Democrats of the mid 19th Century were conservatives, akin to the Republican Party of today, while the Republicans of the mid 19th Century were liberals, akin to the Democratic Party of today. Thus the Confederacy's Democratic president, Jefferson Davis, was a conservative (with libertarian leanings); the Union's Republican president, Abraham Lincoln, was a liberal (with socialistic leanings).

☞ For a more complete portrait of Forrest, see my books:
- *A Rebel Born: A Defense of Nathan Bedford Forrest*
- *Nathan Bedford Forrest: Southern Hero, American Patriot - Honoring a Confederate Icon and the Old South*
- *The Quotable Nathan Bedford Forrest: Selections From the Writings and Speeches of the Confederacy's Most Brilliant Cavalryman*
- *Give 'Em Hell Boys! The Complete Military Correspondence of Nathan Bedford Forrest*

☞ For those interested in the truth about the War for Southern Independence, see my books:
- *Everything You Were Taught About the Civil War is Wrong, Ask a Southerner! - Correcting the Errors of Yankee "History"*
- *Honest Jeff and Dishonest Abe: A Southern Children's Guide to the Civil War*
- *The Quotable Jefferson Davis: Selections From the Writings & Speeches of the Confederacy's First President*
- *The Old Rebel: Robert E. Lee As He Was Seen By His Contemporaries*
- *The Quotable Robert E. Lee: Selections From the Writings and Speeches of the South's Most Beloved Civil War General*
- *The Constitution of the Confederate States of America Explained: A Clause-by-Clause Study of the South's Magna Carta*
- *The Quotable Stonewall Jackson: Selections From the Writings and Speeches of the South's Most Famous General*
- *Abraham Lincoln: The Southern View - Demythologizing America's Sixteenth President*
- *Lincolnology: The Real Abraham Lincoln Revealed in His Own Words - A Study of Lincoln's Suppressed, Misinterpreted, and Forgotten Speeches and Writings*
- *The Unquotable Abraham Lincoln: The President's Quotes They Don't Want You to Know!*
- *Encyclopedia of the Battle of Franklin: A Comprehensive Guide to the Conflict That Changed the Civil War*
- *The McGavocks of Carnton Plantation: A Southern History - Celebrating One of Dixie's Most Noble Confederate Families and Their Tennessee Home*
- *Carnton Plantation Ghost Stories: True Tales of the Unexplained from Tennessee's Most Haunted Civil War House!*

INTRODUCTION

Amazingly, there are still some who do not understand how it is possible to love the great Confederate General Nathan Bedford Forrest. These are individuals, however, who do not know him, have not studied him, have not "spent time with him." They have had their minds filled with so much anti-South propaganda, Yankee mythology, and Northern lies concerning Forrest and Lincoln's War that they actually have no idea who he really was and how important he is to American history.

In reality Forrest was the polar opposite of the negative image of him long portrayed in pro-North "history" books. This is why the more one learns about him the more one appreciates him. For as it turns out he is not only a laudable role model for people of all ages and races, he is the very embodiment of the American dream. Thus, to help counter the numerous unwarranted, irrational, and erroneous attacks on my cousin, this, my fifth book on the General, is devoted to those characteristics which make him admirable, even loveable.

Though I subtitled this work "99 Reasons To Love Nathan Bedford Forrest," this was only for practicality's sake. There are, of course, far more than 99 reasons to venerate him. Nonetheless, I believe that this book will prove to be an ideal starting point for anyone wanting to become more informed about the General, as well as learn the truth about him, what he stood for, and why he left the Union with Tennessee and donned Confederate gray in June 1861.

An honest reading will indeed bring about a fuller understanding of what traditional Southerners have always known: Forrest was an extraordinarily ingenious, courageous, and humane individualist who fought for constitutional freedom against Northern tyranny and big government, and who contributed much to the development of America. As such, he deserves our admiration, esteem, awe, and yes, our love.

Lochlainn Seabrook, SCV
Franklin, Williamson County, Tennessee
July 13, 2012, Forrest's 191st birthday

FORREST!

99 Reasons To Love
Nathan Bedford Forrest

Reason 1

Forrest survived a fatherless and impoverished childhood on America's early Western frontier.[1]

Reason 2

After the death of his father William Forrest in 1837, fifteen year old Forrest worked long hours at various menial jobs in order to support his now one parent family—a thirteen-person clan that included his pregnant mother, three sisters, six brothers, and one of his aunts.[2]

Reason 3

At this time, Forrest, the eldest son, also took over supervision of his mother's farm as well as her business affairs.[3]

Reason 4

While young Forrest was running his mother's homestead, he attended school in a rustic one-room log cabin.[4]

Reason 5

Due to his heavy work load and serious family responsibilities, teenage Forrest was forced to sacrifice furthering his education. As a result, he received only six months of formal schooling.[5]

Reason 6

A true pioneer from birth, as a youngster Forrest made his own clothing, as well as various articles of clothing for his family members.[6]

Reason 7

Young Forrest's efforts eventually turned his mother's farm into a profit-making venture for the first time, something not even his own father had been able to achieve.[7]

Reason 8

At age sixteen Forrest hunted down and killed a mountain lion that attacked his mother and his aunt, thereby saving his family from further danger.[8]

Reason 9

In 1841 twenty year old Forrest joined a Mississippi militia and traveled to Texas to help fight for the republic's independence from Mexico.[9]

Reason 10

In 1842 twenty-one year old Forrest became a junior partner in his Uncle Jonathan Forrest's livestock trading company, helping to turn it into a thriving business.[10]

Reason 11

In 1845 twenty-four year old Forrest defended his Uncle Jonathan from an attack by a gang of four individuals. Though Jonathan died during the fight, Forrest was able to kill two of the assailants and put the other two in prison.[11]

Reason 12

For single-handedly defending his uncle against four thugs, and for helping clean up the streets of the city, Forrest was elected constable of Hernando, Mississippi, by the grateful townspeople.[12]

Reason 13

Despite being a rough and tumble, unlettered frontiersman, Forrest's native smarts and highly ambitious nature gained him the opportunity to marry into a well-to-do, influential Southern family: the Montgomerys.[13]

Reason 14

Forrest had two children with his wife Mary Ann, the first, his son William, who grew up to serve in the Confederate army during Lincoln's War.[14]

Reason 15

In 1851 Forrest moved his new family to Memphis, Tennessee, where he started up numerous successful businesses, supporting his wife and children, employing hundreds of local whites and blacks, and helping to fuel the local economy.[15]

Reason 16

In 1857 Forrest saved a local ruffian, John Able, from an angry mob of 3,000. For his gallantry he was elected alderman of the city of Memphis.[16]

Reason 17

By 1859, at the age of thirty-eight, Forrest had become a multimillionaire, one of the largest plantation owners in Tennessee, and one of the wealthiest men in the South—worth an estimated $40 million in today's currency.[17]

Reason 18

Forrest's wealth allowed him to take care of an invalid younger brother (injured in the Mexican-American War), and put his other brothers through college, a privilege that he himself had been denied.[18]

Reason 19

Forrest, who rose from dire poverty to fabulous wealth, lived a life that was a true rags-to-riches story. He achieved the American Dream like few before or after him.[19]

Reason 20

A well-known Memphis slave-trader, Forrest closed down the business and freed nearly all of his servants in 1859,[20] despite the fact that slavery was then at its peak profitability.[21] This was five years before Lincoln issued his fake and illegal Final Emancipation Proclamation (in 1863), and seven years before the ratification of the Thirteenth Amendment (in 1865) which then and only then officially ended slavery across the U.S.[22]

Reason 21

Forrest was a man's man who proudly proclaimed himself the personal defender and protector of women and children.[23]

Reason 22

Though he was from the tobacco growing, whiskey producing state of Tennessee, Forrest did not smoke cigarettes or drink alcohol, considering them unhealthy vices of the worst kind.[24]

Reason 23

Forrest personally eschewed womanizing and carousing, regarding them both as detestable evils.[25]

Reason 24

Forrest was a traditional Southerner who enthusiastically embraced the customs, rituals, beliefs, and traditions of the Old South.[26]

Reason 25

Politically speaking Forrest was a right-wing Conservative who fell into the category of what we would today call a Libertarian. As such he was an advocate of small government, states' rights, self governance, personal liberty, capitalism, modest taxes, free trade, individualism, and strict constitutionalism.[27]

Reason 26

Forrest was a proud gun owner and hunter who stood squarely behind the Second Amendment.[28]

Reason 27

Forrest was an old-fashioned chivalrous Southern gentleman.[29]

Reason 28

Unlike Lincoln and most other Northerners,[30] Southerner Forrest loved the U.S. Constitution. Later, after Southern secession, he embraced the C.S. Constitution with equal fervor.[31]

Reason 29

Completely shattering the Yankee image of Forrest as a "lifelong unregenerate criminal," the truth is that he never spent a single night in a jail or a prison—before, during, or after Lincoln's War.[32]

Reason 30

During Forrest's brief seven year period as a slave owner and trader, he was well-known for his humanitarian and charitable treatment of his servants, such as refusing to sell them to cruel owners and reuniting divided slave families—even if it meant taking a financial loss.[33]

Reason 31

Forrest was obsessively clean, elegant, and neat in appearance, to the point where some called him "foppish."[34]

Reason 32

Even after Lincoln's election in November 1860, Forrest remained a strong Unionist, speaking out publicly against secession.[35]

Reason 33

In the Spring of 1861, by which time it had become patently clear that Lincoln not only intended to further abuse the South and her rights but also alter the Constitution to benefit the North, Forrest became an ardent disunionist and a fiery champion of secession.[36]

Reason 34

Shortly after Tennessee's secession in early June 1861, Forrest volunteered to serve in the Confederate army and fight for God and country.[37]

Reason 35

Forrest often outfitted, equipped, clothed, fed, and armed his soldiers using his own money, in one case advancing his quartermaster the modern equivalent of $450,000 from his personal bank account for cavalry supplies. (He was never reimbursed by the Confederacy, of course, because Lincoln illegally destroyed the C.S. government in April 1865.)[38]

Reason 36

At the beginning of Lincoln's War, Forrest enlisted forty-five of his remaining black servants in his cavalry. While some operated merely as teamsters, cooks, and hostlers, he trained and drilled a number of them who he then recruited to serve as armed soldiers.[39]

Reason 37

Forrest assigned seven of his black soldiers to act as his own personal armed guards, positions they maintained throughout the entire duration of Lincoln's War. (If Forrest was truly a "vile and physically abusive racist," as his uneducated critics refer to him, one wonders how he could have slept peacefully for four years knowing that each night seven black soldiers were standing over him with loaded weapons.)[40]

Reason 38

Forrest also enlisted an additional twenty free Southern blacks in his command, making a total of sixty-five black soldiers in his cavalry in all.[41] (This was at a time when Lincoln was prohibiting the enlistment of both blacks and Indians in the U.S. army.)[42]

Reason 39

Forrest's black soldiers were integrated directly into his cavalry, fighting side-by-side with his white soldiers.[43] (This practice was in stark contrast to that seen in the U.S. armies, where Lincoln and his Yankee officers enforced strict racial segregation of their white and black troops.)[44]

Reason 40

While Lincoln was busy thinking up ways to stall and even avoid issuing the Emancipation Proclamation,[45] Forrest promised his forty-five "enslaved" black soldiers their freedom at war's end, whether the South won or not.[46]

Reason 41

Halfway through Lincoln's War, Forrest was by now so fed up with the "slavery issue" and so impressed with the valor of his forty-five black servant soldiers, that he decided to emancipate them there and then. This occurred shortly after the Battle of Chickamauga, fought September 18-20, 1863.⁴⁷ Lincoln's fraudulent Final Emancipation Proclamation (which actually did not free a single slave) was issued four months later, on January 1, 1863.⁴⁸

Reason 42

Like most other Confederate officers (such as Robert E. Lee, Stonewall Jackson, and Patrick R. Cleburne), Forrest advocated freeing black servants who volunteered to fight in the Rebel army and navy. (Though blacks had fought *unofficially* with and for the Confederacy since the very first day of Lincoln's War,[49] tragically, Forrest's idea was not *officially* adopted by the C.S. government until March 1865, too late to have any impact on the outcome of the conflict—which ended a mere four weeks later on April 9.)[50]

Reason 43

Forrest was a born farmer, adventurer, and frontiersman who possessed a deep and abiding love for the great outdoors, Nature, Mother Earth, and animals.[51]

Reason 44

Forrest, who literally grew up on horseback, had a special relationship with the equine species.[52] During liberal Lincoln's unconstitutional and bloodthirsty invasion of the South, Forrest's warhorses were often as famous as he was. By order of Forrest himself, one in particular, Roderick, was buried with full military honors after the celebrated gelding died during the Battle of Thompson's Station, which took place on March 5, 1863.[53]

Reason 45

During Lincoln's War Forrest fought bravely and stoically for constitutional freedom in some fifty battles, skirmishes, and engagements throughout Tennessee, Kentucky, Alabama, Georgia, and Mississippi.[54]

Reason 46

Forrest never once surrendered his men in any battle during Lincoln's War.[55]

Reason 47

Forrest won every battle he led, except for the Battle of Selma, fought April 2, 1865, and this was only because: 1) many of his soldiers at the time were greenhorns, 2) he was outmanned nearly three to one, and 3) a Confederate courier carrying his battle plans was captured previous to the fight.[56]

Reason 48

Until the Battle of Selma Forrest was the only Rebel commander in the Western Theater who had never been defeated.[57]

Reason 49

During the four long years of Lincoln's illicit and unnecessary War, Forrest personally killed thirty foreign invaders (Yankee soldiers) who had come South to murder him and his family and take over his country.[58]

Reason 50

During Lincoln's War Forrest had thirty-nine horses shot out from underneath him—underscoring the severity of the battles he was involved in.[59]

Reason 51

During Lincoln's War Forrest survived being shot at 179 times.[60]

Reason 52

During Lincoln's War, from June 1861 to May 1865, Forrest fought the modern equivalent of four consecutive tours of duty, taking only one brief furlough to visit his wife.[61] Additionally, he was severely wounded four times.[62] Had he fought in World War II, he would have received a staggering four Purple Heart medals.

Reason 53

In defense of his country and the Constitution, during Lincoln's War Forrest personally attacked and wounded hundreds of Union soldiers.[63]

Reason 54

During Lincoln's War Forrest seized and destroyed tens of millions of dollars worth of Yankee supplies, helping to grind down the North.[64]

Reason 55

During Lincoln's War Forrest captured, in total, some 31,000 Yankee prisoners—uninvited foreigners who had no right trespassing on Southern soil.[65]

Reason 56

During Lincoln's War, at one time or another, nearly 50,000 (or 5 percent of the total number of) Confederate soldiers came under Forrest's command, including some 100 organizations, such as regiments, battalions, and batteries.[66]

Reason 57

At the start of Lincoln's War Forrest promised the mothers, wives, and sisters of his men that he would protect them,[67] and never ask them to do anything he himself would not do.[68]

Reason 58

The inventor of the 19th-Century's version of the "shock and awe" form of cavalry attack, Forrest's brilliance on the battlefield outraged, dazzled, confused, and stunned his Yankee foes, from the lowliest privates (who quaked in fear at the mere mention of his name) to the highest Union officers, including Grant and Sherman.[69] And as is clear from the *Official Records*, Forrest even got under Lincoln's skin.[70]

Reason 59

At the Battle of Shiloh (April 6-7, 1862), as he rode brazenly out across the battlefield, Forrest was shot in the side by a Union soldier. Though the wound was extremely painful, nearly severing his spine, he ignored the injury and instead reached down and grabbed his assailant by the collar, hoisted him onto the back of his horse, and used the astonished Yank as a human shield while he galloped off the field to safety.[71]

Reason 60

At the Battle of Murfreesboro (July 13, 1862) Forrest routed and captured a Union army twice the size of his own. The General's victory, achieved without artillery and with a command of poorly equipped men, caused a sensation across both the South and the North. Forrest called it "my forty-first birthday present."[72]

Reason 61

On July 21, 1862, Forrest and his men accidently stumbled upon a party at President Andrew Jackson's former Nashville home, the "Hermitage," where they joined in the celebration of the one-year anniversary of the Confederate win at the Battle of First Manassas.[73]

Reason 62

At the Battle of Paducah (March 25, 1864), Forrest rode his 2,500-man cavalry 100 miles in a mere fifty hours—an astonishing feat then or today.[74]

Reason 63

During Lincoln's War Forrest made life for the Yankees a living hell by wreaking devastation on their supply lines, tearing up miles of railroad, bombing train stations, burning Union blockhouses, stockades, and sawmills, dynamiting bridges and trestles, destroying culverts and viaducts, cutting their telegraph wires, disabling their field artillery, firing their warehouses, sinking their supply ships, transport ships, and gunboats, and capturing their supply trains, depots, and garrisons.[75]

Reason 64

Forrest came up with a brilliant plan to win the War for Southern Independence: close down the Tennessee and Mississippi Rivers, the Union's two main supply routes. (Tragically, the idea was ignored in Richmond, much to the detriment of the Confederacy. After the War U.S. General Ulysses S. Grant admitted that the South would have won within one year if a protraction strategy, as proposed by Forrest, had been implemented by the Confederacy in early 1865.)[76]

Reason 65

After Lee's capitulation at Appomattox on April 9, 1865, Forrest refused to surrender his men.[77] Instead, he planned to carry on the fight by joining up with other Confederate forces in the Western Theater. (When Jefferson Davis was captured at Irwinville, Georgia, on May 9, 1865, he had been on his way to meet with Forrest in an attempt to continue the Confederacy.)[78]

Reason 66

Contrary to pro-North "history" books, during battle Forrest treated all captives, white, black, free, and bonded, as prisoners of war.[79] On some occasions, in obedience to the C.S. Constitution's "Fugitive Slave Law"[80] (patterned on a clause in the U.S. Constitution that was supported by Lincoln),[81] Forrest, legally and responsibly, had runaway servants returned to their owners.[82]

Reason 67

Humanitarian Forrest nearly always gave his Yankee opponents a fighting chance in battle, often issuing them a demand for unconditional surrender ("to prevent the further effusion of blood") even before the first shot was fired. (Those who refused this generous offer inevitably paid a terrible price.)[83]

Reason 68

Though Forrest has been charged by the North with ordering a "massacre" at the Battle of Fort Pillow (April 12, 1864), the truth is that he actually prevented any unnecessary bloodshed by issuing strict orders to his men before and during the battle. Two of his privates disregarded the orders. He had the first one arrested and the second one shot. Later, a U.S. government investigation into the Battle of Fort Pillow found no evidence that Forrest had committed any crimes during the conflict and absolved him of any wrongdoing.[84]

Reason 69

Forrest tried to avert the disaster that would come to be called the Battle of Franklin II (fought November 30, 1864), by recommending to his commander John Bell Hood that he be allowed to use his cavalry to flank the Yankees. Hood refused the idea, as well as all other recommendations offered by his officers, and instead ordered a full frontal assault across a two-mile wide open plain. As a result, 1,750 Confederates died and thousands more were injured in the doomed attack that day.[85]

Reason 70

Forrest ended the War as the only man on either the Confederate or the Union side to rise from private to lieutenant general—just one rank shy of full general.[86]

Reason 71

Though Lincoln's War bankrupted Forrest, through sheer hard work and determination he was able to launch (or assume leadership of) numerous businesses and get back on his feet financially. Eventually this allowed him to purchase real estate and start up large scale farming again.[87]

Reason 72

After the War, during so-called "Reconstruction," Forrest rehired hundreds of his former black servants, all who enthusiastically came back to work for him—this time as free laborers.[88] The always lenient Forrest gave them generous pay advances and allowed them to carry guns and knives (both at work and at home), much to the alarm and anger of the racist Yankee Reconstruction officers in charge of overseeing Forrest's farm.[89]

Reason 73

Shortly after Lincoln's War Forrest forgave the Union and began doing business with former Yankee officers, a noble and altruistic attempt to reconcile with the North and resuscitate the battered Southern economy.⁹⁰

Reason 74

Contrary to Yankee mythology, Forrest did not found the Ku Klux Klan in December 1865, nor was he its first leader (known as the "Grand Wizard"). There is not even any definitive evidence that he was a member. He did, however, passionately endorse the anti-Yankee, relief and aid society, whose original mission was to maintain the peace and assist war widows, orphans, and Confederate veterans—*of all races*.[91] His support of the pro-South organization included an all-black KKK chapter in Nashville.[92]

Reason 75

In 1868 Forrest told blacks that he was the true friend of the Negro, then asked them to stand with him against the North's duplicitous, race-baiting Loyal Leagues. "We have always stood by you," he rightly told them.[93]

Reason 76

In 1869 Forrest announced that he wanted to bring more blacks from Africa to Dixie, stating that they are "the finest workers the South has ever known."[94]

Reason 77

In the late 1860s, after Forrest founded the Selma, Marion, and Memphis Railroad, he hired some 400 blacks; not just as common workers, but as architects, engineers, conductors, and foremen—jobs still closed to blacks in the ultra racist North at the time.[95]

Reason 78

In 1871, two years after Forrest personally closed down the Ku Klux Klan (it had served its original purpose and was by then no longer necessary),[96] he was questioned before a U.S. government committee investigating the KKK, which found him completely innocent of any misconduct associated with the organization.[97]

Reason 79

In the 1870s Forrest publicly denounced white racism, began campaigning for black civil rights, and said he much preferred associating with Southern blacks than white scallywags and carpetbaggers.[98]

Reason 80

In the 1870s Forrest suggested that the Southern states hire Chinese and Japanese immigrants in order to help rebuild the prostrate South.[99]

Reason 81

In 1873 Forrest donated $5,000 ($100,000 in today's currency) to the founding of Nashville's esteemed Vanderbilt University.[100]

Reason 82

Only a decade earlier a confirmed Yankee slayer, on May 30, 1875, Forrest displayed true character and magnanimity when he led a Confederate ceremony at Elmwood Cemetery in Memphis to decorate the gravestones of the Union dead buried there.[101]

Reason 83

On July 4, 1875, Forrest gave a speech before the Independent Order of Pole Bearers, the forerunner of the modern NAACP (now widely considered a racist hate group—even by many blacks).[102] During his address Forrest said that whites and blacks are "brothers and sisters," and that he would do all he could "to bring about harmony, peace, and unity" between the races.[103]

Reason 84

After a lifetime of "sinnin'" (cussing, gambling, and fighting), Forrest converted to Christianity in November 1875, happily joining his wife's Presbyterian Church in Memphis.[104]

Reason 85

In his last years Forrest had his lawyer drop all of his lawsuits, even though he could have easily won them. In doing so he personally lost millions of dollars while sparing his adversaries both misery and possible financial ruin.[105]

Reason 86

Just before his death Forrest willed most of his estate to Southern charities dedicated to helping Confederate veterans as well as war widows and orphans of all races.[106]

Reason 87

During his final public speech on September 21, 1877, Forrest opened by mentioning the soldiers of his command first because, as he said, "I love them best."[107]

Reason 88

Forrest was a devout family man, father, and husband, marrying only once, and remaining faithfully with his spouse Mary Ann for his entire life. Indeed, his last words were: "Call my wife."[108]

Reason 89

According to eyewitnesses, of the 20,000 people who attended Forrest's funeral on October 31, 1877, fully one-third of them were African-Americans, all who came to grieve and pay their final respects to the great Confederate chieftain. (Compare this to Abraham Lincoln's Northern funeral, where blacks were barred from attending altogether.)[109]

Reason 90

During battle Forrest would "give quarter" to any man, white or black, who requested it.[110]

Reason 91

Forrest was called "the greatest revolutionary leader of the Confederacy" by one of his contemporaries.[111] One of his foes, Yankee war criminal General William T. Sherman, declared Forrest "the most remarkable man the Civil War produced on either side."[112] Rebel General Robert E. Lee said of Forrest: "He accomplished more with fewer troops than any other officer, Confederate or Union."[113]

Reason 92

Forrest, whose battlefield tactics and strategies are still studied in military schools around the world, has often been described as an "untutored military genius."[114]

Reason 93

Forrest was a free-thinking nonconformist and Southern individualist who never imitated anyone, thought for himself, and could lead but could not be led.[115]

Reason 94

Forrest conceived most of his battle plans on the hoof and often overran and captured Yankee commands without a single shot being fired.[116]

Reason 95

Forrest ignored the accepted "West Point" method of fighting, and instead invented his own, culled from a lifetime of experiences as a mountaineer, farmer, and frontiersmen.[117]

Reason 96

Forrest was always ready to face the same risks as his men, even leading them directly into battle (unusual for a military officer).[118] He not only shared his ever faithful soldiers' hazards and difficulties, he often slept on the ground alongside them and ate the same food they did.[119]

Reason 97

Forrest's formulas for winning battles were simple: 1) be there first with the most men; 2) hit 'em hard and fast; and 3) never back down from a fight.[120]

Reason 98

Forrest, the consummate trickster, could "brag 'n bluff" his way through any fight (even if greatly outnumbered), and hide a thousand Confederate soldiers and their horses in the bushes off a road just yards from passing Yankees without being detected.[121]

Reason 99

Widely known in his time for his heroism, self-reliance, brilliance, strong work ethic, generosity, inventiveness, personal cleanliness, courage, tenacity, and love of liberty, to those who are familiar with the real Forrest, to this day his name is synonymous with the South, the Confederacy, political conservatism, racial harmony, and the Constitution.[122] He remains both the personification of the Southern gentleman and the "spiritual comforter" of the Southern people, even recently replacing Robert E. Lee as the South's most popular general.[123]

NOTES

1. Seabrook, NBF, p. 20.
2. Seabrook, ARB, pp. 194-195.
3. Seabrook, ARB, p. 195.
4. Seabrook, ARB, p. 194.
5. Seabrook, ARB, pp. 195-196.
6. Seabrook, ARB, p. 195.
7. Seabrook, ARB, pp. 195-196.
8. Seabrook, ARB, pp. 181-182.
9. Seabrook, ARB, pp. 196-197.
10. Seabrook, ARB, pp. 197-198.
11. Seabrook, ARB, pp. 198-199.
12. Seabrook, ARB, pp. 199-200.
13. Seabrook, ARB, pp. 201-203.
14. Seabrook, ARB, p. 204. Forrest's second child, Frances Ann "Fanny" Forrest," died in childhood.
15. Seabrook, ARB, pp. 204-205.
16. Seabrook, ARB, pp. 205-206, 564.
17. Seabrook, ARB, pp. 206-207.
18. Seabrook, ARB, p. 204.
19. Seabrook, ARB, p. 547.
20. Seabrook, ARB, p. 206.
21. Seabrook, ARB, pp. 185, 220.
22. Seabrook, ARB, pp. 219-220.
23. Seabrook, ARB, pp. 208, 582.
24. Seabrook, ARB, p. 208.
25. Seabrook, ARB, p. 208.
26. Seabrook, ARB, pp. 208-209.
27. Seabrook, ARB, pp. 7, 37, 75-76, 208-209
28. Seabrook, ARB, pp. 164, 521-522.
29. Seabrook, ARB, pp. 200, 209, 480, 543, 548.
30. See Seabrook, ALSV, p. 66.
31. Seabrook, ARB, pp. 37-38, 165-166, 208, 257, 389, 442.
32. Seabrook, ARB, pp. 209, 541.
33. Seabrook, ARB, pp. 149, 213-215, 220-221.
34. Seabrook, ARB, p. 221.
35. Seabrook, ARB, pp. 26, 208-209.
36. Seabrook, ARB, p. 257.
37. Seabrook, ARB, p. 257.
38. Seabrook, ARB, pp. 257-258.
39. Seabrook, ARB, pp. 26, 144, 152, 259, 305-306, 368.
40. Seabrook, ARB, pp. 26, 144.
41. Seabrook, ARB, pp. 259, 504.
42. Seabrook, L, pp. 333, 654. See also p. 864.
43. Seabrook, ARB, pp. 101, 306, 341, 368, 460.
44. Seabrook, ARB, pp. 51, 93, 101, 155, 306, 341, 368, 385, 460.
45. Seabrook, TUAL, pp, 108-116; Seabrook, ALSV, passim; Seabrook, L, pp. 634-697.
46. Seabrook, ARB, pp. 258-259.
47. Seabrook, ARB, pp. 156, 259-260.
48. Seabrook, L, pp. 634-697.
49. Seabrook, ARB, p. 305.
50. Seabrook, ARB, p. 574.
51. Seabrook, ARB, pp. 176, 177, 179, 180.
52. Seabrook, ARB, pp. 177, 515.
53. Seabrook, ARB, pp. 290-291.
54. Seabrook, ARB, p. 558.
55. Seabrook, ARB, passim; NBF, passim.
56. Seabrook, ARB, pp. 417-420.
57. Seabrook, ARB, p. 541.
58. Seabrook, ARB, p. 542.
59. Seabrook, ARB, p. 542.
60. Seabrook, ARB, p. 542.
61. Seabrook, ARB, p. 570.
62. Seabrook, ARB, p. 542.

63. Seabrook, ARB, p. 542.
64. Seabrook, ARB, p. 542.
65. Seabrook, ARB, p. 542.
66. Seabrook, ARB, p. 542.
67. Seabrook, ARB, p. 284.
68. Seabrook, GEHB, p. 290.
69. Seabrook, ARB, pp. 509-546.
70. Seabrook, ARB, p. 293.
71. Seabrook, ARB, pp. 284-285.
72. Seabrook, ARB, p. 285.
73. Seabrook, ARB, p. 286.
74. Seabrook, ARB, p. 285.
75. Seabrook, ARB, pp. 320-321.
76. Seabrook, ARB, pp. 300-304.
77. Seabrook, ARB, pp. 421-422.
78. Seabrook, ARB, pp. 299-300.
79. Seabrook, ARB, pp. 329, 384.
80. Seabrook, TCCSAE, p. 118. See also U.S. Constitution, Article Four, Section Two, Clause Three.
81. Seabrook, ARB, p. 102.
82. Seabrook, ARB, pp. 337-338, 384, 534.
83. Seabrook, ARB, pp. 329, 490, 522-523.
84. Seabrook, ARB, pp. 327-388.
85. Seabrook, ARB, pp. 393-395.
86. Seabrook, ARB, pp. 541, 574.
87. Seabrook, ARB, pp. 431-437.
88. Seabrook, ARB, p. 433.
89. Seabrook, ARB, pp. 433-434.
90. Seabrook, ARB, pp. 432-433.
91. Seabrook, ARB, pp. 437-451.
92. Seabrook, ARB, p. 441.
93. Seabrook, ARB, p. 457.
94. Seabrook, ARB, pp. 457-458.
95. Seabrook, ARB, pp. 436-437.
96. Seabrook, ARB, pp. 442-443, 451.
97. Seabrook, ARB, pp. 448-450.
98. Seabrook, ARB, pp. 456-457.
99. Seabrook, ARB, p. 458.
100. Seabrook, ARB, p. 453.
101. Seabrook, ARB, p. 456.
102. See Seabrook, ALSV, p. 341.
103. Seabrook, ARB, pp. 459-460.
104. Seabrook, ARB, p. 455.
105. Seabrook, ARB, pp. 455-456.
106. Seabrook, ARB, p. 461.
107. Seabrook, ARB, p. 464.
108. Seabrook, ARB, p. 465.
109. Seabrook, ARB, p. 12.
110. Seabrook, ARB, p. 460.
111. Seabrook, ARB, p. 509.
112. Seabrook, ARB, pp. 11-12.
113. Seabrook, ARB, p. 8.
114. Seabrook, ARB, p. 509.
115. Seabrook, ARB, p. 512.
116. Seabrook, ARB, pp. 512-514.
117. Seabrook, ARB, p. 510.
118. Seabrook, ARB, pp. 383, 499.
119. Seabrook, ARB, pp. 427, 527.
120. Seabrook, ARB, pp. 518, 542.
121. Seabrook, ARB, pp. 518, 521.
122. Seabrook, ARB, passim.
123. Seabrook, ARB, pp. 200, 549.

BIBLIOGRAPHY
✷ And Suggested Reading ✷

Seabrook, Lochlainn. *Nathan Bedford Forrest: Southern Hero, American Patriot: Honoring a Confederate Icon and the Old South.* 2007. Franklin, TN: Sea Raven Press, 2010 ed.

———. *Abraham Lincoln: The Southern View.* 2007. Franklin, TN: Sea Raven Press, 2010 ed.

———. *The McGavocks of Carnton Plantation: A Southern History - Celebrating One of Dixie's Most Noble Confederate Families and Their Tennessee Home.* 2008. Franklin, TN: Sea Raven Press, 2011 ed.

———. *A Rebel Born: A Defense of Nathan Bedford Forrest, Confederate General, American Legend.* 2010. Franklin, TN: Sea Raven Press, revised 2011 ed.

———. *Everything You Were Taught About the Civil War is Wrong, Ask a Southerner!* 2010. Franklin, TN: Sea Raven Press, revised 2012 ed.

———. *Lincolnology: The Real Abraham Lincoln Revealed In His Own Words.* Franklin, TN: Sea Raven Press, 2011.

———. *The Quotable Jefferson Davis: Selections From the Writings and Speeches of the Confederacy's First President.* Franklin, TN: Sea Raven Press, 2011.

———. *The Unquotable Abraham Lincoln: The President's Quotes They Don't Want You To Know!* Franklin, TN: Sea Raven Press, 2011.

———. *The Quotable Robert E. Lee: Selections From the Writings and Speeches of the South's Most Beloved Civil War General.* Franklin, TN: Sea Raven Press, 2011.

———. *The Old Rebel: Robert E. Lee As He Was Seen By His Contemporaries.* Franklin, TN: Sea Raven Press, 2012.

———. *The Quotable Nathan Bedford Forrest: Selections From the Writings and Speeches of the Confederacy's Most Brilliant Cavalryman.* Franklin, TN: Sea Raven Press, 2012.

———. *Give 'Em Hell Boys! The Complete Military Correspondence of Nathan Bedford Forrest.* Franklin, TN: Sea Raven Press, 2012.

———. *Honest Jeff and Dishonest Abe: A Southern Children's Guide to the Civil War.* Franklin, TN: Sea Raven Press, 2012.

———. *Encyclopedia of the Battle of Franklin: A Comprehensive Guide to the Conflict That Changed the Civil War.* Franklin, TN: Sea Raven Press, 2012.

———. *The Constitution of the Confederate States of America Explained: A Clause-by-Clause Study of the South's Magna Carta.* Franklin, TN: Sea Raven Press, 2012.

———. *The Quotable Stonewall Jackson: Selections From the Writings and Speeches of the South's Most Famous General.* Franklin, TN: Sea Raven Press, 2012.

MEET THE AUTHOR

JOCHLAINN SEABROOK, winner of the prestigious Jefferson Davis Historical Gold Medal for his "masterpiece" *A Rebel Born: A Defense of Nathan Bedford Forrest,* is an unreconstructed Southern historian, award-winning author, Forrest scholar, and traditional Southern Agrarian of Scottish, English, Irish, Welsh, German, and Italian extraction. An encyclopedist, lexicographer, musician, artist, graphic designer, genealogist, and photographer, as well as an award-winning poet, songwriter, and screenwriter, he has a thirty year background in historical nonfiction writing and is a member of the Sons of Confederate Veterans, the Civil War Trust, and the National Grange.

(Illustration © Tracy Latham)

Due to similarities in their writing styles, ideas, and literary works, Seabrook is referred to as the "American ROBERT GRAVES," after his cousin, the prolific English writer, historian, mythographer, poet, and author of the classic tomes *The White Goddess* and *The Greek Myths.*

The grandson of an Appalachian coal-mining family, Seabrook is a seventh-generation Kentuckian, co-chair of the Jent/Gent Family Committee (Kentucky), founder and director of the Blakeney Family Tree Project, and a board member of the Friends of Colonel Benjamin E. Caudill. Seabrook's literary works have been endorsed by leading authorities, museum curators, award-winning historians, bestselling authors, celebrities, noted scientists, well respected educators, renown military artists, esteemed Southern organizations, and distinguished academicians from around the world.

Seabrook has authored some thirty popular adult books specializing in the following topics: the American Civil War, pro-South studies, Confederate biography and history, the anthropology of religion, comparative mythology, genealogical monographs, Goddess-worship (theology), ghost stories, the paranormal, family histories, military encyclopedias, etymological dictionaries, ufology, social issues, syncretistic analysis of the origins of Christmas, and cross-cultural studies of the family and marriage.

His seven children's books include a Southern children's guide to the Civil War, a dictionary of religion and myth, a rewriting of the King Arthur legend (which reinstates the original pre-Christian motifs), two bedtime stories for preschoolers, a naturalist's guidebook to owls, a worldwide look at the family, and an examination of the Near-Death Experience.

Of blue-blooded Southern stock through his Kentucky, Tennessee, Virginia, West Virginia, and North Carolina ancestors, he is a direct descendant of European royalty via his 6th great-grandfather, the EARL OF OXFORD, after which London's famous Harley Street is named. Among his celebrated male Celtic ancestors is ROBERT THE BRUCE, King of Scotland, Seabrook's 22nd great-grandfather.

The 21st great-grandson of EDWARD I "LONGSHANKS" PLANTAGENET), King of England, Seabrook is a thirteenth-generation Southerner through his descent from the colonists of Jamestown, Virginia (1607).

The 2nd, 3rd, and 4th great-grandson of dozens of Confederate soldiers, one of his closest connections to the War for Southern Independence is through his 3rd great-grandfather, ELIAS JENT SR., who fought for the Confederacy in the Thirteenth Cavalry Kentucky under Seabrook's 2nd cousin, Colonel BENJAMIN E. CAUDILL. The Thirteenth, also known as "Caudill's Army," fought in numerous conflicts, including the Battles of Saltville, Gladsville, Mill Cliff, Poor Fork, Whitesburg, and Leatherwood.

Seabrook is also related to the following Confederates and other 19th-Century luminaries: ROBERT E. LEE, MARY ANNA RANDOLPH CUSTIS (General Lee's wife), STEPHEN DILL LEE, JOHN SINGLETON MOSBY, STONEWALL JACKSON, NATHAN BEDFORD FORREST, JAMES LONGSTREET,

JOHN HUNT MORGAN, JEB STUART, P. G. T. BEAUREGARD (codesigner of the Confederate Battle Flag), JOHN BELL HOOD, ALEXANDER PETER STEWART, EDMUND W. PETTUS, ABRAHAM BUFORD, JOHN B. WOMACK, THEODRICK "TOD" CARTER, ARTHUR M. MANIGAULT, JOSEPH MANIGAULT, CHARLES SCOTT VENABLE, THORNTON A. WASHINGTON, JOHN A. WASHINGTON, JOHN H. WINDER, GIDEON J. PILLOW, STATES RIGHTS GIST, EDMUND WINCHESTER RUCKER, HENRY ROOTES JACKSON, JOHN C. BRECKINRIDGE, MARK PERRIN LOWREY, HUGH ALFRED GARLAND JR., TYREE HARRIS BELL, ROBERT FRANKLIN BECKHAM, JESSE JOHNSON FINLEY, WILLIAM ANDREW QUARLES, LEONIDAS POLK, ZACHARY TAYLOR, SARAH KNOX TAYLOR (the first wife of JEFFERSON DAVIS), RICHARD TAYLOR, DAVY CROCKETT, DANIEL BOONE, MERIWETHER LEWIS (of the Lewis and Clark Expedition) ANDREW JACKSON, JAMES K. POLK, ABRAM POINDEXTER MAURY (founder of Franklin, TN), WILLIAM GILES HARDING, ZEBULON VANCE, THOMAS JEFFERSON, GEORGE WYTHE RANDOLPH

(grandson of Jefferson), JOHN THOMAS LEWIS PRESTON, FELIX K. ZOLLICOFFER, FITZHUGH LEE, NATHANIEL F. CHEAIRS, JESSE JAMES, FRANK JAMES, ROBERT BRANK VANCE, CHARLES SIDNEY WINDER, JOHN W. MCGAVOCK, CARRIE (WINDER) MCGAVOCK, DAVID HARDING MCGAVOCK, LYSANDER MCGAVOCK, JAMES RANDAL MCGAVOCK, RANDAL WILLIAM MCGAVOCK, FRANCIS MCGAVOCK, EMILY MCGAVOCK, WILLIAM HENRY F. LEE, LUCIUS E. POLK, MINOR MERIWETHER (husband of noted pro-South author Elizabeth Avery Meriwether), ELLEN BOURNE TYNES (wife of Forrest's chief of artillery, Captain John W. Morton), South Carolina Senators PRESTON SMITH BROOKS and ANDREW PICKENS BUTLER, and famed South Carolina diarist MARY CHESNUT.

Seabrook's modern day cousins include: PATRICK J. BUCHANAN (conservative author), REBECCA GAYHEART (Kentucky-born actress), SHELBY LEE ADAMS (Letcher County, Kentucky, portrait photographer),

BERTRAM THOMAS COMBS (Kentucky's fiftieth governor), EDITH BOLLING (wife of President Woodrow Wilson), and actors ROBERT DUVALL, REESE WITHERSPOON, LEE MARVIN, and TOM CRUISE.

Born with music in his blood, Seabrook is an award-winning, multi-genre, BMI-Nashville songwriter and lyricist who has composed some 3,000 songs (250 albums), and whose original music has been heard on TV and radio worldwide. In 2012 his poignant ballad *That's My Girl*—recorded and produced by JOHN CARTER CASH (son of JOHNNY CASH and executive producer of the five-time Academy Award-winning film *Walk the Line*)—was selected for inclusion in the film *Cowgirls N' Angels*, starring BAILEE MADISON, JACKSON RATHBONE, and JAMES CROMWELL.

A musician, producer, multi-instrumentalist, and renown performer—whose keyboard work has been variously compared to pianists from HARGUS ROBBINS and VINCE GUARALDI to ELTON JOHN and LEONARD BERNSTEIN—Seabrook has opened for groups such as the EARL SCRUGGS REVIEW, TED NUGENT, and BOB SEGER, and has performed privately for such public figures as President RONALD REAGAN, BURT REYNOLDS, and Senator EDWARD W. BROOKE.

Seabrook's cousins in the music business include: JOHNNY CASH, ELVIS PRESLEY, BILLY RAY and MILEY CYRUS, PATTY LOVELESS, TIM MCGRAW, LEE ANN WOMACK, DOLLY PARTON, PAT BOONE, NAOMI, WYNONNA, and ASHLEY JUDD, RICKY SKAGGS, the SUNSHINE SISTERS, MARTHA CARSON, and CHET ATKINS.

Seabrook lives with his wife and family in historic Middle Tennessee, the heart of the Confederacy, where his conservative Southern ancestors fought valiantly against liberal Lincoln and the progressive North in defense of Jeffersonianism, constitutional government, and personal liberty.

LOCHLAINNSEABROOK.COM

If you enjoyed Mr. Seabrook's *Forrest! 99 Reasons To Love Nathan Bedford Forrest* you will be interested in his other works on the General:

A REBEL BORN: A DEFENSE OF NATHAN BEDFORD FORREST
NATHAN BEDFORD FORREST: SOUTHERN HERO, AMERICAN PATRIOT
GIVE 'EM HELL BOYS! THE COMPLETE MILITARY CORRESPONDENCE OF N. B. FORREST
THE QUOTABLE NATHAN BEDFORD FORREST

Available from Sea Raven Press and wherever fine books are sold.

www.ingramcontent.com/pod-product-compliance
Lightning Source LLC
LaVergne TN
LVHW041546070426
835507LV00011B/959